The Right Staff
D. A. Spence

Books maybe purchased at:
www.therightstaffbook.com

Cover & Interior Design: Diren Yardimli
Cartoon Artist: David Fletcher
Editors: Kim Smith & Steffannie Alter

ISBN: 978-0-6484383-0-4

© 2019 by Debra Spence. *All rights reserved.*

No part of this book may be reproduced in any written,
electronic, recording, or photocopying without written
permission of the publisher or author.
The exception would be in the case of brief quotations
embodied in the critical articles or reviews and pages
where permission is specifically granted
by the publisher or author.

Although every precaution has been taken to verify the
accuracy of the information contained herein, the author
and publisher assume no responsibility
for any errors or omissions.
No liability is assumed for damages that may result from
the use of information contained within.

THE RIGHT STAFF

D.A. SPENCE

Dedication

I want to thank all my staff, the good, the bad, the ugly but most of all the fantastic employees that inspired me.

I dedicate this book to my son, Bryce that I bestowed the gift of Dyslexia too. May this book be his inspiration to write also?

Foreword

By Dr Anthony Grace

For me, the early part of this century can be described as, "the employees search for purpose." People don't want to *just* work for a company, they want to work for a company that has a clear and meaningful purpose. More so, the organisation's strong sense of purpose ideally aligns with the employee's own values. *Debra Spence* has written a comprehensive book on the complex environment that is the modern-day workplace. Beginning with a story of a harrowing ordeal she experienced on a Monday, Debra recounts how she came to the realisation that the classic advice about staffing was not setting her up for success. These traditional expectations were only adding to the stress. The solution: a simple and straightforward human resource system that can be easily applied to any small to medium sized business.

It begins with an appreciation of human energy as a form of capital. Hiring the right employees at the right time becomes a truly valuable resource. This point is consistent with literature from a myriad of leading academic journals where the following point is stressed: human capital is an essential and sustained source of competitive advantage for any organisation. And while these skills, experiences, ideals, values, attitudes and competencies of people within the company are never 'owned' by the company, they can be harnessed. Chapter 2 focuses on a very important, often unmentioned aspect harnessing employee talent: if managers are required to get the most out of their people, why are they mostly perceived in a negative way. Debra writes, "it is time to change the way people view their bosses." She goes on to describe in detail four positive leadership styles: the control enthusiast, the visionary, the coach, or the commander. Understanding which type you might be requires honest self-reflection, but it is important to do to gain further clarity on how the personalities of both boss and staff play a significant role in harnessing human capital. Furthermore, chapter four sets out three easy steps to determine your own "boss blueprint".

This book also contains a wealth of insight into other employment considerations: how to write a perfect job description (chapter 6); the seven sins of recruiting and a solution in the form of a three-tiered selection process (chapter 7); how to 'let go' and empower employees to do what they were employed to do (chapter 8); the reflective mirror method (chapter 9); the attitude to have when a good employee leaves you (chapter 10); Fostering a great team environment (chapter 11); How to incentivise employees (chapter 12). The following pages certainly do contain a wealth of information relevant to the ins and outs of staffing.

The Right Staff is an important book for understanding today's volatile employment environment. It is a must for those of us who need a guiding beacon to help navigate through the ever-changing employment landscape. It is an enjoyable read with great anecdotes and great case studies. One worth mentioning, described in chapter 11, is Google's project Aristotle. The researchers had a simple mandate: determine what makes a team effective? Five criteria were found to contribute to effective teamwork, these included psychological safety and impact. Employees crave to work in a place where they feel psychologically and emotionally safe, not threatened. Furthermore, as we progress through this century, it becomes more and more evident that most employees desperately want to make a meaningful impact. *The Right Staff* is a book that delivers simple and straightforward advice on how to get the most out of human capital, but more so, how to set up the organisation, yourself, and your staff for success.

Dr Anthony Grace, PhD
Ducere Global Business School
University of Canberra, Australia

Contents

Introduction: Death by Mondays 13

Chapter 1: Heart Starter for Your Business
   The benefits of hiring employees for your business 23

Chapter 2: Trip, Fall and Stabbed in the Back
   It is time to change the way people view their bosses 33

Chapter 3: Mirror, Mirror on the Wall
   Why your personality affects who you should hire 41

Chapter 4: Who's the Fairest in the Land?
   Blueprint—establishing your boss style 65

Chapter 5: Your Team, Your Rules
   Your team needs to know how to work
   within your leadership style. 75

Chapter 6: Get What you Really Want
   Defining your needs 89

Chapter 7: Time to Slice, Dice, and Select
   The Three-Tier Selection Process 97

Chapter 8: Take Action and Let Go
   Let them 'do' and become part of the team 117

Chapter 9: It's Me, Not You!
   Breaking up can be easy 125

Chapter 10: It's You, Not Me
   It is never about the money 143

Chapter 11: I Have Your Back if You Have Mine
   It is all about teamwork 153

Chapter 12: Sharing your Toys
   Pay, incentives and pay rises 163

Chapter 13: Back to the Future
   Recap and where to go for help 177

Death by Mondays

"Good morning, Sir. Would you like to start the week with coffee or CPR?"

Did you know the most common time of day to have a **heart attack** is between 4 am and 10 am on a **Monday**? Work, business and life can throw you curve balls which in hindsight can prove to be a comical and catalyst to changing out lives. Here is my story of a life changing Monday that turned my business life upside down.

It was a typical Monday drive in peak-hour traffic when suddenly my head began thumping with unbelievable pain. 'I don't get headaches,' I muttered.

The last time I'd had a headache had been five or six years prior when I'd decided to go cold turkey and give up my ten-coffee-a-day habit.

The lights turned green and I pressed the accelerator. It took only a moment to realise that my left arm had gone numb and limp.

What was happening to me? Panic started to take over as I felt my left leg going numb as well. I figured I was either dreaming or about to die.

There was nowhere to pull over, but through my panic, I remembered that the local ambulance station was just up the road. If I could get myself there, I would—just maybe—survive.

By the time I got to the ambulance station, the whole left side of my body had gone limp. The last thing I remember was sliding down the station front door, hitting it with my head, praying that someone would hear my knock.

I came to in the ambulance long enough to speak to one of the two officers who was giving me an injection. I explained that my head hurt and that the left side of my body was numb and unresponsive.

I was feeling lost and scared, and I could hear the other officer talking on the phone. 'Yes, Mr Spence, we will contact you with updates on your wife. Mr

Spence, she's just regained consciousness...I will call you back.'

The world started to spin and go black again and my thoughts turned to my husband, who was working 1200 kilometres (745 miles) away on a construction site and was not due home for another week. Then the world disappeared again.

I awoke to find that I was strapped into a head brace. At least my head had stopped pounding, but I still could feel pressure under my left eye and still couldn't move my left side.

I was trying to count my blessings, that at least I was conscious and alive. A nurse came to the side of my bed and explained that they were checking to see whether I'd had a stroke. She said they had given me some medication to relax me and relieve the pain. For a couple of hours I drifted in and out of consciousness as we waited for the CAT scan results.

In the meantime, my husband had rung our cosmetic beauty clinic to notify the employees that I had been rushed to the hospital. He was informed that the business manager was due to arrive and that she would be filled in on the emergency situation. Later, he told me that he had breathed a sigh of relief and thought that the business was going to be okay, enabling him to concentrate on getting home to my side.

Several hours after the CAT scan, the doctor came in and asked how I was. I explained that I had a small thumping headache, but my left side had some movement back. The doctor proceeded to administer the standard reflex test, flashing a light in both eyes and then use a little hammer all over my body. How was this going to make me feel better? Especially since every time my body moved, he would make more notes in his chart. I was far from relaxed.

He continued to scribble for a little while longer without making any comment or eye contact. I was starting to think that it was better to get hit with that tiny hammer than to endure this awkward silence. He looked up from his notes. He asked, 'Are you under a lot of stress?'

The doctor verified that there was no brain haemorrhage; however he wanted me to take the next week off and get some rest. After I was discharged, I sat in the hospital cafeteria and waited for my dad to pick me up. I was feeling a little stupid and lonely, sipping on my cup of tea in solitude, when my phone vibrated, it was a text from our business manager: 'Can you bring toilet paper next time you come in?'

I just starred at the text message, trying to comprehend the content, as I was shock from what I had read. Had I'd hired a manager who couldn't arrange for either herself or one of the other employees to go up the road to the general store and buy some toilet paper? The shop was less than a 200 metres (218 yards) walk up the hill! Shaking my head slowly as tears welled up in my eyes I knew something had to change, and it had to change fast, or next time I would be carried out of the hospital in a box. How did I get into this position with a manager like this and how was I going to get out of this mess?

I sat in silence and started to piece together the journey that had led to this event. I realised that for many years, I had listened to the advice from human resources managers, organisational psychologists and recruiting officers on how to hire, manage and fire employees. The classic advice I heard usually included:

1. Businesses need a variety of personality styles—diversification is the key.
2. A boss needs to bend and be flexible to their employees' needs.
3. It is the boss's job to motivate their employees and make them happy.

4. It is the boss's fault if the employees are not doing their jobs correctly.
5. It is the boss's fault if employees are not satisfied.

I found that these traditional expectations on employers were not helping me to build a successful business or a great team. Instead, these excessive expectations were creating an undue amount of work and high stress levels—it was killing me.

I had to find a better approach to hiring and firing employees. The approach had to be easy, stress-free and effective. But the first thing I had to do was summon up the courage to sack the manager and another employee who was destroying my business and me.

This event was the catalyst that I needed to turn a struggling business with numerous employee issues into an award-winning, successful and stress-free environment. All it took was throwing out everything I knew about Human Resources and developing a simple and straightforward human resources system that could be applied to any small or medium sized business.

Take-Home Point

No business is worth your life, even if it is your 'why' for living.

If you find yourself in a bed you do not like, don't lie in it; get up and re-make it as you will be surprised how much better life can be.

Heart Starter for Your Business

The benefits of hiring employees for your business

*A ship in harbour is safe—
but that is not what ships are built for.*

JOHN A. SHEDD

At some point, every business owner will have to decide whether to hire an employee or not. Let's face it: having staff can be seen as a hassle and extra work. When you go to any networking or business function, you'll hear business owners tell stories about the nightmares that their employees are causing them.

Many business owners are stretched across multiple business tasks to 'save' money and grow their business. The idea of recruiting, hiring and managing employees becomes just another torturous thing that a business owner must do.

If you try to do everything yourself and be a Lone Wolf, you may find yourself working 80–100 hours a week. When you stop, so will your income. You will be your own worst employee and work yourself to death. You will burn out at some point, and when you do, you will go out of business. This is the downside to being a Lone Wolf.

Business owners are often time-poor and may be financially limited; therefore they value both money and time. Often, the business owners' thought process goes something like this—how much of my time is going to be used in explaining to the employee what to do, I might as well do the job myself and avoid the pain of telling the employee what to do.

A Lone Wolf business owner believes it is quicker and cheaper to perform the task themselves rather than employ someone to do the task for them. However, the reality it is more important that the task that is to be performed be valued based on the how much it can reduce cost to the business or produce income for the business. This is called opportunity cost/income potential and when a task is valued in this framework, then a business owner can appreciate the potential of having employees perform these tasks.

"Yeah, my boss is going to work me into an early grave too, and I'm self-employed!"

To Clean or Not to Clean

> *Think about hiring a cleaner so that you are free to generate sales instead of cleaning your premise. If hiring the cleaner costs $30 per hour and it takes four hours to clean, you are paying $120 for this task to be completed.*
>
> *It may seem like you're losing $120 but think about the opportunity that being free from this cleaning task could mean to a business. In those four hours, you could make sales calls, see paying customers, produce products, plan the advertisement layout for your next marketing campaign or complete any other income-producing tasks. Who knows how much money you may be losing by spending those four hours cleaning? The opportunity cost/income potential could be far more than the $120 paid to a cleaner.*

Half of all new businesses fail within the first five years, and only about one-third survive more than ten years. The rates of entry and exit are highest for businesses without employees, the Lone Wolf businesses. Medium-sized businesses with more than 15 employees enjoy the lowest business failure rate.

Three-quarters of midsize companies are still in operation five years after they launch. The likelihood that a business survives the start-up phase increases with the number of employees they hire. The quicker your business can hire employees, the better chance that it has to grow in size, and the more likely for that business to be successful.

THE $$$ VALUE OF HAVING STAFF

$5 MILLION 20 OR MORE STAFF
$100K WITH 1-4 STAFF
$50K NO STAFF

Hiring an employee can also improve the income potential of the business owner. Most businesses that have no employees (the Lone Wolf business) will only make an annual net profit after tax of approximately $50,000, and 10% of those businesses make a loss. Business that hires a single employee will have a net profit after tax over $100,000. Medium to large business can make a profit up to $5 million. Employees are the key to your cash flow, profitability and longevity.

If improving your business's chance of survival and increasing profits is not enough of a motivator to start hiring, consideration of the seven benefits listed below should make you want to stop being a lone wolf business:

1. External encouragement—a cheer squad for your business vision creating a sense that you're not pursuing this business goal alone.
2. Employees can provide expertise and skills that you may not have.
3. Increased problem-solving potential—remember, a problem shared is problem halved.
4. Many hands make light work. Complementary skills allow you to reduce your physical hours and increase your productivity.
5. Employees provide accountability to keep going.

6. Employees help to increase the passion, energy and drive need in business.
7. Employees can provide honest feedback.

Although having employees is beneficial, it's not the solution for every problem. There are other potential dangers when trying to build up staff. Hiring too early may create cash-flow problems. A worker who has nothing to do can add stress to your business. However, if you hire too late, you run the risk of employing the wrong person because you are desperate to fill the position quickly. If you go for just anybody, you'll usually end up with the wrong person. Desperation makes for disaster.

> *Don't hire an accountant when you need an administrator.*
>
> *Don't hire a doctor when you need a nurse.*
>
> *Hire the best person for the task to be completed*

When you have a task that needs to be done, stop and ask yourself—do I need to hire an employee, or is there another way I can get the task completed? Today, we have many services that can be outsourced or done by freelancers and other self-employed business people. You can even hire a 'virtual' administrative assistant. If you only need someone for a few hours per week or month, you can contract this task out.

Timing is very important, but so is an understanding of the specific skill set needed for the task at hand. If you don't know exactly what a task requires to be completed correctly, you may hire someone whose skill set doesn't match your needs. Never hire out of laziness. Make sure that you have a long-term need for the employee before you decide to hire, otherwise contract this task out.

Take-Home Point

The right employee = Longevity, Cash Flow and Profit

Having an employee is the key to creating a company that will grow and survive

Desperation = Disaster

Hire at the right time and the right person for you and the task.

Trip, Fall and Stabbed in the Back

It is time to change the way people view their bosses

> *When life is viewed as good,*
> *a bad day is easily absorbed.*
>
> NEIL MAXWELL

Have you noticed how often bosses are portrayed negatively, both in fiction and real life? Dictator, Terminator, Power Tripper, Unwanted Buddy and Shiny Object Chaser. There are many articles, books and popular movies about bad bosses, from *9 to 5* to *Horrible Bosses*. There is huge amount of literature on how to survive and handle the various different kinds of 'bad boss'. There are even articles on how to stay sane until you can find a new job. These negative connotations and belief systems have an adverse effect on business and on how employees and employers interact.

"I think you'll find it takes more than a fake halo to make you seem like a good boss."

With all these negative stereotypes, is it any wonder that employees don't always deliver their best? These biases about bosses can contribute to a toxic work environment. This type of toxicity makes employees feel uncomfortable, unappreciated and undervalued. It can create an air of mistrust and stir up unfounded hostility towards an employer. It is not the way to build a winning business. A positive perspective is a secret power that can free us from a world of hurt, pain, struggle and negative views of other people.

I have never met a businessperson that has set out to be a bad boss. The first step is to move away and reject these negative labels. The second step is to find positive employer imagery and labels. It is time to find a positive description of bosses that encourages a constructive work environment and attracts the right employees for your boss leadership style.

There are four basic styles of positive leadership for a business: Control Enthusiast, Visionary, Coach and Commander. Below is a description of each of these styles; see if you can relate to any or some of them.

Control Enthusiast—you like to be involved in every aspect of an employee's work. You like having constant feedback from your employees to enable you to make any minor adjustment needed. This is how you ensure that your business is on track to success. You like giving detailed work directions, frequently checking progress and reviewing your employee's work. This doesn't mean that you don't trust your staff, but rather that you feel calmer when you have the entire set of details at your hand.

Visionary—if the Control Enthusiast focuses on the details, the Visionary is all about the big picture. You see the overview and look at the business's potential. You have many ideas about which direction the company can take. You do not do details unless you really need to. You are results-oriented. You are not concerned about the 'how' but more concerned with the 'why' and when a task will be done. You reward on completed tasks, not for attendance.

Coach—you know what each employee is capable of. You constantly want to draw out the best from each of them. You know their strengths, their weaknesses and push them to grow. You expect only their best work in return for bringing them to their full potential. You assign tasks to the employee that you see has the talent and skills to complete it well.

Commander—the company's success is driven by you alone, and not from people that you employ. Staff are there to do a job and to do it correctly first time. You are able to identify and rectify mistakes quickly to prevent a larger problem. You don't have time for a company mindset driven by empathy or compassion. Business is business, and home is home. You believe that your job is to be at the helm of your business, and you manoeuvre your employees into position with direct and precise instructions.

Each one of these employer styles takes a different approach to running a business. Hopefully one of these leadership styles, or a , or a combination of styles has resonated with you.

Take-Home Point

Positive Boss Image will change the work environment.

Cultivate a positive image for your leadership style.

Mirror, Mirror on the Wall

Why your personality affects who you should hire

Sometimes you've got to be able to listen to yourself and be okay with no one else understanding.

CHRISTOPHER BARZAK

Being a Lone Wolf can be satisfying, you control everything, you reap the rewards of what you sow but you also carry the burden on your own shoulders. If you want your business to go to the next level, grow and prosper, you will need to hire the right staff at the right time. To help you with this, you need to understand what type of boss you are and the type of employees that suit your leadership style. This way, your employees will be an asset, not a liability, to you and your business.

Being an employer is very different from being a manager or an employee. It's important to understand the differences to ensure that you have a clear vision of the tasks a boss carries out.

1. Business owners create a vision for the business and its staff, whereas managers develop goals for employees to achieve.
2. Bosses are change agents who navigate the various obstacles that may arise in creating their vision, whereas managers maintain the status quo of the current business.
3. Bosses take risks, whereas managers control risks in order to maintain the everyday operations of the company.
4. Bosses are big-picture thinkers who help determine the business's course. Managers, in contrast, focus on the day-to-day workings of the business.
5. Bosses build relationships with all stakeholders—including customers, suppliers, manufacturers, employees and government bodies—whereas managers develop systems and processes around those stakeholders' needs and requirements.

Transitioning from a Manager to a Boss

I have always been a natural leader; captain of my team, who rose quickly through the ranks to management positions in most jobs. To me, becoming a boss seemed like it was going to be a no-brainer. I could not have been more wrong.

My first experience of being a boss was when I decided to buy a restaurant. Restaurants have the highest failure rate of any form of business. But failure was not an option, and I was going to be the best boss EVER. I was going to be friendly, caring, understanding, flexible and always there to help my staff.

I hired people based on their stories. If the candidate told me about difficulties or gave me hard luck stories, I would hire them over someone that was better qualified to do the task. I hired a chef that had lost two babies and was about to have another child. I did not even check to see if he could cook the items on menu. I hired a young woman that was paying her way through school so she could get into university, but I did not check to see if she could actually wait on tables. I was a complete sucker for a sob story. I did not hire employees on merit or capabilities or my leadership style.

> *There were many reasons why this business failed, but the most significant reason was that I did not know what type of boss I was and what staff would suit my style or if an employee could even do the task I had hired them to do.*

In order to understand who you should hire, you have to look at how you lead. Find out what type of boss you are. Most small business owners would say that 'All they want' was a carbon copy of themselves, but ask yourself, do want an employee that is all over the place and doing 300 things at once (because this is what most new business owners are like.)? The answer would be NO. However, would you hire the version of yourself that is passionate about your business, is excited about the future of your company and focused on the big picture? The answer would be a resounding 'Yes, of course!'

As a foundation on the type of boss you will be, the first step is to look at how you learn, teach and lead others. Understanding yourself as a learner enables you to also understand how you solve problems and what influences you when making decisions. When in business you need to work smarter and not harder, so by understanding your learning style, you can better gather, process and take action upon information when it is delivered in your preferred form.

Everyone has their own way of learning and interacting with the world around them. Howard Gardner's theory of multiple intelligences, first outlined in his 1993 book *Frames of the Mind: The Theory of Multiple Intelligences* identified eight ways people solved problems and learnt new information. He posited that regardless of an individual's intellectual level, we all learn though our senses. He further argued that we all have a preferred sense that we use to learn and solve problems. Of the five senses—visual (sight), auditory (hearing), kinesthetic (action and/or feeling-touch), gustatory (taste), olfactory (smell) —the three top senses for learning and problem-solving are visual, auditory and kinesthetic.

The simplest way to understand your learning and problem-solving style is to take note of how you explain or tell a story or how you prefer to learn something new.

Visual people process information with their eyes. They are often the person taking notes so they can see what is being said. They love charts, demonstrations, videos and other visual stimuli. They will need to see the problem to be able to solve it.

Auditory people process information with their ears. They are the ones that are often talking or listening to music or make noise. To solve problems, they need to verbalise it first.

Kinaesthetic people process information with their hands. They learn by touching and moving; they need external stimulation or movement. When solving a problem, they tend to scan the problem to get the big picture first and then focus on the details.

Understanding your learning and problem-solving style will enable you to lead, communicate with and manage your employees more effectively. It's important that you're able to swiftly communicate not only what tasks need to be done, but articulate how they should be completed. Time is money, and any shortcut to reducing miscommunication and improving cooperation is worthwhile.

Learning in 40°C (105°F) Degrees and 50 Kilometres (31 Miles) from Town

> *When I was learning to survey for our company, Zentec Surveys, I went out in the field with the head surveyor, my husband William. I learn through sight/kinaesthetic, while my husband learns primarily through auditory channels with a little mix of kinaesthetic. When*

my husband explained the survey instruments and the history of their usage, I tuned out right away. I just wanted to set up the instrument and start doing the survey.

He went into detail about the various parts inside of the survey Total Station while he pulled it out of the case to mount it on the tripod. Again, his words just sounded like a dull buzz to me.

Then, he turned to me. 'Your turn to take over,' he said. I looked at him, dumbfounded. I had no idea what to do.

'Were you not listening to me?' William sternly asked me. William tried explaining another three times, pushing buttons on the instrument as he talked.

I was frustrated to the point of screaming. 'How am I supposed to learn this when all you do talk and do everything? I'm a sight-action person so how do think is the best way for me to I learn this?'

After three attempts to get William to stop talking and allow me to start learning my way, it all got too much for me. I stormed off and started walked toward the town 50 kilometres away.

That day taught us both a valuable lesson on how to teach and how we learn.

Identifying your learning style is the first step in becoming self-aware and understanding your strengths and weaknesses both as a person, and a leader. It's through recognising your learning style that you can develop a deeper understanding of your leadership style. This information will help you understand what type of employees you need and how to find them. At the end of this chapter is a learning and problem-solving style test. This is the first step in understanding and helping you to identify your individual Boss Blueprint.

Let's look at what type of boss you are in the next step of formulating your Boss Blueprint.

We covered the four basic positive types of leadership/boss styles in the previous chapter. You may have identified with either the Control Enthusiast, Visionary, Coach or Commander and to find the employees that will help you build your business vision, we need to dive a little deeper than these four general boss descriptions.

Self-reflection is the hardest part of becoming a boss, I guarantee it, but it is like ripping off a band-aid. Do it quickly, and you will be so glad that you did.

Getting to know yourself honestly and thoroughly will help ensure that you hire the right staff. Ask yourself—do you feel calm and in control when you have your finger on the whole control panel? Are you more at ease and feel calm when you are going with the flow yet still flexible to change direction as your business requires it? Is your style more from the sidelines, positioning your employees in the best possible situation to move your business forward to the winning line, or do you feel at home when at the helm of the ship and instructing your employees to steer your business to success? Are you a list-maker or a spreadsheet person, or do you like to keep everything in your head and then dish out the information in increments?

Your personality is one of the factors that pilot your behaviour and actions. Opening ourselves up to learning about ourselves will inspire personal growth and can improve our understanding of how we interact with our world, especially in the business world.

There are several ways to find out what kind of boss you are. Firstly, ask friends and family for honest reviews of yourself. Ask them to share the good, the bad and the ugly of your behavioural habits. Make a note of the typical behaviours and traits that arise in these conversations.

The Sledgehammer

My friends say I'm a sledgehammer; don't ask me for my view or solution to a problem unless you want a blunt response. I don't use flowery language or beat around the bush; I tell it like it is. My friends know this about me, and so sometimes they explicitly ask me to listen but not to give my opinions or advice.

> *Some people see this as a negative trait, and some people don't cope well with such bluntness. It's best for me to be aware of this before making hiring decisions. Your traits are what make YOU.*
>
> *I own my sledgehammer trait, as it has served me well in many instances. But if a characteristic is not serving you well and is causing you hardship, then it is up to you to choose to change that trait.*
>
> *As a leader in your business, you need to be aware of your traits and own them.*

If you are looking for a way to gain unbiased and honest reflection, you can take personality tests, especially ones that are designed to highlight your leadership and management tendencies. There are two easy, free tests that I particularly like to use for understanding myself and my personality traits, the '16Personalities' test and the 'DOPE' personality test. The DOPE test was highlighted in the movie *The Other Guys* featuring Will Ferrell and Mark Wahlberg, in which Wahlberg's character constantly expressed that he was a peacock—website links can be found at the end of this chapter.

The 16Personalities test will help you pinpoint

your leadership style. This test is scientifically based on the Carl Jung and Myer Briggs psychological personality tests, but the difference is that it does not incorporate Jungian concepts of cognitive functions. It has five personality aspects.

1. Mind—how you interact with your surroundings.
2. Energy—defines how you see the world and process the information.
3. Nature—explains how you make decisions and cope with emotions.
4. Tactics—determines how you approach work, planning and decision-making.
5. Identity—defines how confident you are in your abilities and choices.

This test can help explain many facets of your personality and help determine why you do the things that you do. It enables you to accept your strengths and manage your weakness, as well as pinpoint tasks for which you will need to hire employees to do. This test will help you in starting to think about which employees will work best with your leadership style. This insight allows us to own our traits and hire employees without guilt and stress.

The 16Personalities test highlighted why I avoid some business tasks like the plague and gravitated towards other task without much coaching. For example I would, and still do, avoid bookkeeping at all costs yet am happy to sit for hours trying to find a way to teach a complex idea in a simple format.

This test can highlight whether you should be a day-to-day manager once the business passes its initial start-up phase, or whether you should step aside and employ a manager to take on the everyday business operations.

The insights from the 16Personalities test are fascinating, but if you are wanting something a little simpler and straightforward, then take a look at the DOPE personality test, which defines your personality using one of four types of bird.

The DOPE personality Test is a fun little test to help you break down your inner being and provide basic insight into you and your leadership style. It is a useful tool that I like to have in my human resource toolbox to better understand the people that I'm working with. The four bird types identified by this personality test are:

1. Eagle—bold and decisive. You can be dominant, stimulated by challenges and be direct and very decisive. You are a natural achiever.
2. Dove—peaceful and friendly. You are people-orientated and very loyal. Friendly, hardworking and great team player.
3. Owl—wise and logical. You are mathematical and methodical and can be a bit of a perfectionist. You love details.
4. Peacock—showy and optimistic. You love talking and being the centre of attention. You have a wealth of passion and enthusiasm and optimism.

It is no surprise that I was labelled a peacock when I took this test. I never see the negatives in any of my business ventures until it hits me in the face. Not seeing negatives can be somewhat a hazard but I prefer to see the world full of options and not obstacles.

This simple test is also helpful in the hiring process, as you are not going to hire a bookkeeper that is not predominantly an owl personality or a customer liaisons officer without some dove qualities.

Both these tests are to help you to understand and be more informed about your personality traits and leadership style. They will help you see what will make your business work better and be more successful.

For the reader that finds these personality tests not to their liking, or you just don't want to do the exercises, at the end of this chapter there is a list of all general personality traits that you can use to formulate a list that represents you. You could even copy the list and give it to your current staff, family and friends to get their views on your traits and highlight the common traits they see in you.

Take-Home Point

Accept yourself and all your various traits without apology. If you don't like a trait, it's your job to change it.

Learning and Problem-Solving Style Test—by D R Clark

Read each statement carefully and score the statement using the scoring system below. Try not to change an answer once you have selected one.

Once you have completed the test, total your score in the spaces provided below

1 = Almost Never Applies

2 = Applies Once in a While

3 = Sometimes Applies

4 = Often Applies

5 = Almost Always Applies.

Section one—visual	Score
I take written notes and/or draw mind maps.	
When talking to someone else, I have a difficult time understanding those who do not maintain good eye contact with me.	
I make lists and notes because I remember things better if I write them down.	
When reading a novel, I pay a lot of attention to passages that help me to picture the clothing, description, scenery, setting, etc.	
I need to write down directions so that I can remember them.	
I need to see the person I am taking to in order in order to keep my attention focused on the subject.	

When meeting a person for the first time, I notice the style of dress, visual characteristics, and neatness first.	
When I am at a party, one of the things I love to do is stand back and observe the people.	
When recalling information I can see it in my mind and remember where I saw it.	
If I had to explain a new procedure or technique, I would prefer to write it out.	
In my free time I am most likely to watch television or read.	
If my boss has a message for me, I am most comfortable when she sends a memo.	
Total for visual	

Section two—auditory	Score
I read out loud or move my lips to hear the words in my head.	
When talking to someone, I have a difficult time understanding those who do not talk or respond with me.	
I do not take a lot of notes, but I still remember what was said. Taking notes often distracts me from the speaker.	
When reading a novel, I pay a lot of attention to passages involving conversations, talking, speaking, dialogues, etc.	

I like to talk to myself when solving a problem or writing.	
I can understand what a speaker says, even if I am not focused on the speaker.	
I remember things easier by repeating them over and over.	
When I am at a party, one of the things I love to do is talk in-depth about a subject that is important to me with a good conversationalist.	
I would rather receive information from the radio, rather than read a newspaper.	
If I had to explain a new procedure or technique, I would prefer talking about it.	
With my free time I am most likely to listen to music.	
If my boss has a message for me, I am most comfortable when he or she calls me on the phone.	
Total for auditory	

Section three—kinaesthetic	Score
I am not good at reading or listening to directions. I would rather just start working on the task or project at hand.	
When talking to someone, I have a difficult time understanding those who do not show any kind of emotional or physical support.	

I take notes, doodle, and/or make mind-maps, but I rarely go back and look at them.	
When reading a novel, I pay a lot of attention to passages revealing feelings, moods, action, drama, etc.	
When I am reading, I move my lips.	
I often exchange words, such as places or things, and use my hands a lot when I can't remember the right thing to say.	
My desk appears disorganised.	
When I am at a party, one of the things I love to do is enjoy the activities such as dancing, games, and totally losing myself in the action.	
I like to move around. I feel trapped when seated at a meeting or a desk.	
If I had to explain a new procedure or technique, I would prefer demonstrating it.	
With my free time I am most likely to exercise.	
If my boss has a message for me, I am most comfortable when she talks to me in person.	
Total for kinaesthetic	

The section with the highest score will generally by your predominate learning and problem-solving style.

Clark, D R (2013). VAK Learning Styles Survey website link http://www.nwlink.com/~donclark/hrd/styles/vak.html.

Website Links to the personality and leadership traits:

1. 16Personalities test—
   https://www.16personalities.com/
2. DOPE personality est—http://richardstep.com/dope-personality-type-quiz/

General Personality Traits List

Circle the personality traits that resonates with you to formulate your personality trait and leadership style.

Adventurous	Affable	Capable	Charming
Confident	Conscientious	Cultured	Dependable
Discreet	Dutiful	Encouraging	Exuberant
Fair	Fearless	Gregarious	Helpful
Humble	Imaginative	Impartial	Independent
Intelligent	Keen	Meticulous	Observant
Optimistic	Persistent	Precise	Reliable
Trusting	Valiant	Arrogant	Boorish
Bossy	Conceited	Cowardly	Dishonest
Finicky	Impulsive	Lazy	Malicious
Obnoxious	Picky	Pompous	Quarrelsome
Rude	Sarcastic	Self-centred	Slovenly
Sneaky	Stingy	Sullen	Surly
Thoughtless	Unfriendly	Unruly	Vulgar

Who's the Fairest in the Land?

Blueprint—establishing your boss style

> *I am not afraid of storms,*
> *for I am learning how to sail my ship.*
>
> **Louisa May Alcott**

Our personality defines us and how we interact with the world. The last chapter was a step towards understanding your personality and leadership traits. Some of the results from doing the exercises in chapter 3 may have come as a surprise to you, or just confirmed what you already know about yourself. The tests could have highlighted some negative traits that you may wish to modify, but that is up to you to decide on a case-by-case situation. In this chapter we are working towards formulating your individual Boss Blueprint from the personality and leadership traits established by the tests.

Physiologists believe that personality is shaped by early life experiences and tends to stay stable as we develop into adults. It has been shown that personality can change during a lifetime and can be triggered by new life experiences, severe emotional trauma or life-changing events such as becoming a parent. Personality traits are often challenged to change through a catalyst, but the extent of change varies from one person to the next. An emotionally intelligent person does not need a large catalyst to invoke a change, or to bring about greater acceptance of their personality.

Changing traits is like breaking a habit—it takes a considerable amount of conscientious effort over many months, but it can be done if you dedicate yourself. Be sure that any changes you're making are to improve yourself; otherwise you will not be able to sustain the changes. All traits have benefits; so remember the positive aspects of your personality before you attempt to change it.

The Red or Blue Cup

> John is a businessman. He's dependable, dutiful, trustworthy, passionate, and intelligent but also non-communicative, distant and moody. Those latter traits seem negative at first, but they also mean that John doesn't waste time on small talk. When he is distant or moody, everyone leaves him alone, allowing him time to think and solve problems.
>
> The question for John becomes how to manage this trait without alienating co-workers. John decides to use two different colour coffee cups to match his mood. When he comes in the morning and picks the red cup, his employees know that he's busy. When he drinks from the blue mug, they know that he's more receptive to talking. By adapting to his personality traits, John turns them into positive characteristics that allows for better work environment.

Biz Stone, Co-founder of Twitter

> In an article from the June 2015 Harvard Business Review, Biz Stone explained that he recognised that he would never be CEO material. He saw himself in more of a supporting

role, someone who could smooth the business lows and challenges that was required to make Twitter what it is today. Despite being the co-founder of the company with Jack Dorsey, Stone saw himself as creative director and wanted to support the CEOs and have their backs.

This became particularly important when the company made several management changes. Stone worked to help move the employees' loyalty from the previous CEO to the new CEO. He believed his job was to encourage everyone to think about what was best for the company and not just the people in it.

Armed with an understanding of your personality and leadership traits, it is time to dig deeper into finding the right staff for you. There are three easy steps to complete, and then you will have your personalised Boss Blueprint.

This next step will take a little time, but it is well worth it, and it only needs to be done once. This blueprint can be used every time want to hire new employees or fire an employee that doesn't fit well with your business or you.

Establishing your Boss Blueprint

The most significant benefit when completing this exercise is that it establishes who you are as a boss. It tells you what type of employee would benefit from your leadership style and who would not prosper. You will then be ready to hire employees that suit you, and your business, according to the individualised blueprint.

Draw or download the Boss Blueprint table from the, *The Right Staff Book* website – www. therightstaffbook.com.

In the first column, make a list of all the personality traits that define you, as covered in the previous chapter.

Use the second column to list all the benefits you think these traits bring to your business.

In the third column, detail what challenges these same traits bring to your business.

The last two columns are about which employees would benefit or suffer from those traits. Look to the sample Boss Blueprint to help you understand the steps.

Take-Home Point

All traits that can positively contribute to a business's success. Embrace yours

Sample of Boss Blueprint Table

Traits	Benefits to business and staff	Challenges to the business and staff	Type of employee that benefit from this trait	Type of employee that would not benefit
Detail orientated	Detailed instructions and guidelines.	You control everything and thus can cause bottlenecks, as employees wait for your instructions and solutions.	Employees who like everything laid out with no deviations or variables.	Free thinker, streamliner and problems solver. Creative/artistic personality.
'Sledge-hammer'	Cold hard facts.	It can be difficult for people to hear hard truths that are hard to face up to and solve.	Straight shooters who want facts and are not looking for empathy.	Employees who do not want problems solved without empathy and supporting words.

Chapter 5

Your Team, Your Rules

Your team needs to know how to work within your leadership style.

Our diversity is our strength. What a dull and pointless life it would be if everyone were the same.

ANGELINA JOLIE

The major benefit of knowing who you are as a boss is that you can build a team to suit you and your business. This may sound self-centred, but it's your business, your blood and sweat, your dreams and your financial future.

Over the course of many of my business ventures, I have constantly tried to find the formula that would create the best working team. I read books, contracted employment agents and human resource managers and even sought an organisational psychologist's advice. They all said the same thing: to build a robust productive team, you must have a mixture of different personality types. The science behind team diversity is that it enables a team to have an array of different solutions that promote progress within the workplace.

The problem with this philosophy is that it assumes that everyone is equally open to people and can work with everyone; which requires a lot of personal development for many people. As an employer, do you have the skill set, time and money to overcome divisions and build a compatible, complementary team that will cooperate with each other to be productive? Some people may have these skills, but many business owners do not have the time, training or financial means to implement the required action. Many businesses need a team that works, and works now!

When running small or medium-sized business, you want a team that works with you, not one in which there are constant personality clashes that cause you stress and more work. Let's face it, you cannot run a business successfully if it filled with people that you simply cannot get along with. You may have developed biases over your lifetime which could have occurred due to any number of reasons. Your personal biases are yours, recognise them, and own them. However you should work on those traits, privately in your own time, as you may find that these biases are having a negative affect on you and your business.

The over-sharing employee

> *Have you ever been in a situation that you avoid engaging with a co-worker or employee?*
>
> *I had a lovely administration lady she was punctual, courteous but she drove me mad. She would tell me in great detail about her little boy's progress—whether he sniffled 2 or 3 times or how he drew a stick figure in a variety of colours and where he used the colours and on what paper he used. This went on and on and on into the minute detail including details on how he expressed feelings. Her over-sharing did not stop with her little boy, she would talk about every part of her personal life, including her love life, illnesses, even her house cleaning routine.*
>
> *I dreaded the thought of being caught up with her in a conversation.*
>
> *It got to the point that I would avoid her at all costs. I would wait until she left her work station before venturing past her desk to go to the toilet. I would ensure that at meetings she*

was position in the chair furthest away from me. I would send her on unimportant errands to get her away from the office. I even gave her extra days off that she was not entitled too just so I did not have to interact with her.

Unfortunately, one day when I was under the weather and not in a very patient or happy mood, she started over-sharing about her child and I lost it. I screamed at her saying, 'I don't care if your kid is alive or dead just shut up do you work!'

It all ended in tears and she walked out which was understandable as I had handled the situation appallingly. A few days later we sat down over coffee and discussed what happen and with me apologising profusely.

I learnt an important lesson from this incident—over sharing personalities were not a good fit for my Boss Blueprint.

Being in small to medium size business, it is advised that you do not employ someone who you think you would be biased against. Otherwise, you may have to face that bias in a very public and sometimes destructive way. It will make the work environment unpleasant, not just for you but also for all your employees, including the person that you have a negative bias against.

You want employees that add to the business and enable you to build an exceptional team, not people that add to your workload and stress levels. Remember: this is about you and your leadership style and what type of employee that will flourish under your Boss Blueprint.

It is essential to point out that there are workplace laws that make it illegal to discriminate on the basis of race, sex, religion, etc. These very important laws are in place to ensure equal treatment and opportunities for all employees. Seek help and guidance if your behaviour is in anyway discriminatory.

"The next job applicant is wearing green pants. Should I even bother sending him in?"

However, there may be interpersonal traits that will affect who you should choose to be on your team even the ridicules notion of hating green trousers. If your personality type is enthusiastic and optimistic, you're not going to work well with a person that has a victim mentality or a 'doom and gloom' personality. Similarly, if you like people who are honest and very direct, then you likely won't work well with passive-aggressive people that have hidden agendas. Why would you want to have employees that contradict your style and affect your business and other employees?

This is not to say that you should hire clones of yourself, no little mini me's. You will need to hire people that can work with you and complement your style. For example, if you are a non-detail oriented person, you need to hire a person that is detail-oriented to do the task that need this specialisation but has a personality that works with your leadership style.

Many business owners try to do a large variety of tasks and end up wearing a multiple layer of hats to accomplish these tasks. Successful business owners know that if they do not possess the skills or have time to do a task, it is best to have someone else perform them. With this understanding, it is time to work out who you need on your team. You need to work out who to employ, who to contract the work out to along with how you want the task completed to be in alignment with you and your business needs.

Tasks to Your Boss Blueprint Exercise

Draw up a table or download the template from *The Right Staff Book* (www.therightstaffbook.com) and follow these steps. A sample of the table is at the end of this chapter.

Step one

In column 1, list all the tasks that need to be done for your business to be successful. Be very specific about these tasks; don't put down 'administrator' or 'engineer' as these are too generalised. At the end of this chapter there is a small list of various tasks that most small and medium sized business owners need to have performed, which can help you build your own list.

Step two

Estimate how much time it will take you to do these tasks—then double that estimate, as things always take longer than we expect.

Step three

Highlight the task/s that you are constantly putting off or just simply hate doing. Identify ways in which someone other than you could complete those tasks more effectively. These tasks are the first ones for which you should employ someone to do or contract out.

Step four

In Column 2 describe the personality type best suited for each task.

Step five

In Column 3 describe the parameters needed to suit your leadership style.

This step is critical to ensuring that the people you

find to do these tasks will have the personality traits that will fit with your Boss Blueprint.

Take-Home Point

Know who you are and who can work well with you. It's your business, your dream, your future, so make it your team.

A Starting List of Business Tasks		
Product manufacturer	Marketing	Sales representative
Customer support	Business development	Financial analyst
Human resources	Accountant	Bookkeeping
Payroll	Receptionist	Supervising
Trainer	Cleaner	Service provider
Copy writer	Coffee maker	Social and events
Lead generation	Supply sourcing and purchasing	Contract negotiation
Mail and banking	Filtering and answering emails	Packaging

Task to Blue Print Boss Style.

Example of tasks and how they need to be done to meet your leadership style	
Task to be performed	Taxation Requirements, Sales Reports, Accounts Payable, Payroll, Cost of Production
Who	Completed by Bookkeeper/Accountant/Online app.
Estimated Time to complete the Task	15 Hours per week
The personality type best suits this job or task	Compliance orientated, Detail focus, Number focus, not human focus, Historians, Abide by laws and deadlines
Circle the Best Option	Full Time Employee, Part Time Employee Contractor
Example of the Parameters needed to meet general boss style Chapter 2.	Visionary—requires reports only if the sales, expenses and bank account reach a certain level or if an event happens that requires decision from the owner, e.g. BAS lodgement. Coach—explain the financial goals of the company, and have the bookkeeper/accountant set up all the reports required to meet the goals and delivered on time. Commander—task list to be completed daily and detailed reports delivered at various intervals.

Parameters needed to meet your blue print boss style. *Chapter 3 and 4.*	Extrovert—(prefers group activities and is energised by social interaction). Prefers the bookkeeper to present the financial reports to the group/managers in person and not via email. Enthusiastic—(excited about the world and all things new). Present all new laws and requirements as a positive and highlights the benefits of these laws. Sledgehammer—(no fuss or small talk). Presents the facts without over-indulging in the details. Prospective—(good at improvising and spotting opportunities). Flexible, relaxed nonconformists who prefer keeping their options open. Being a non-conformist does not work for the taxation department or for payroll. It is important for your finance team to keep you on track to meet these obligations. Sight/Action person—(learn and teach through pictures and doing the task). Uses graphs and understands how to complete the tasks in the required timeline without constant verbal updates.

Get What you Really Want

Defining your needs

Go for it now. The future is promised to no one.

WAYNE DYER

You are now armed with a list of tasks that you want someone else to complete for you. It does not matter if you are hiring an employee or contracting the task out, the selection process will be the same. Before you start writing up a job description and advertising the position, let's first look at why you need a job description in today's world.

A job description is a written statement that includes roles, responsibilities and functions of a particular position. It also includes the job title, job location, position description, job summary, working conditions and includes the qualifications, skills and experience the person must have to perform the task. The job description enables you, or your recruiters, to hire the person with the competency to do the task required. It also reduces potential legal risks when it comes to performance appraisal or termination.

The downside though, is that a job description tends to lock people in to a very fixed role. Employees may refuse to do tasks that fall outside of their job description, and in today's fast-moving world, flexibility is essential. When you lock an employee into a very specific set of tasks, this discourages innovation, builds artificial walls, and reduces teamwork. All of these factors have a negative effect on your team, reducing productivity and your business profit.

Lesson to avoid

> *This is a story about four people named Everybody, Somebody, Anybody, and Nobody. There was an important job to be done and Everybody was sure that Somebody would do it. Anybody could have done it too, but Nobody did it. Somebody got angry about that, because it was Everybody's job. Everybody thought Anybody could do it, but Nobody realised that Everybody wouldn't do it. It ended up that Everybody blamed Somebody when Nobody did what Anybody could have.*
>
> *Don't let this happen to your business*

The easiest way to reduce the potential downsides of giving employees a job description and still being able to meet your legal requirements is to take the best elements of the job description and put turn it into the Task, Ability and Attitude Brief.

Creating a Task, Ability and Attitude Brief is very easy

Step one

List the skill requirements for each task. This list should include the educational background, skill level and capabilities that a person needs to be capable of performing the task. This way, you can ensure that candidates have the proper qualifications and skills.

For example, a vineyard owner might need a registered taxation accountant with five years' experience to prepare tax returns for wine growers.

Step two

" It says here you work well under pressure."

Necessary abilities and attitude. This element is all about whether the candidate has the ability and attitude to meet your needs and your leadership style. This is why taking the time to do the exercises in the previous chapters will pinpoint which candidates best suits your style. Step 2 can be used to create specific key performance indicators (KPIs) for that task.

For example, if the vineyard owner is a control enthusiast, she might need to find an accountant that is willing to provide constant updates and progress reports at regular intervals.

The Task, Ability and Attitude Brief can now be used to write the position vacant advertisement or to find a contractor/freelancer to carry out the task you require. Below is an example of an advertisement that is built from a Task, Ability and Attitude Brief.

Position Vacant

Looking for a multi-skilled customer-focused person that has the following qualifications, experience and aptitude:

2 years MYOB bookkeeping experience

Ability to use the Zodiac phone system

Competent in MS Mail, MS Word and Excel

Five years' experience in reception and general administration

Understands the importance of answering the phone within five rings

Greets all customers warmly and providing them with a choice of beverages while they wait in reception.

(Continue to list the important tasks this

person needs to do in your business with the attitudes you want them to have.)

It will be during the interview stage that you can test the candidate's ability to meet your needs. In the next chapter we'll delve into how to interview the applicants who respond to the advertised position in order to ensure that you hire the employee with the abilities and attitude that suit the business and your leadership style.

Take-Home Point

The perfect job description.

Use your skills and knowledge to ensure that customers receive the highest quality products and service which meet their needs and wants via the cooperation, interaction and innovation of your fellow workmates, to ensure a healthy profit is obtained for all staff, business owners and stakeholder to share.

Chapter 7

Time to Slice, Dice, and Select

The Three-Tier Selection Process

Death will be a great relief. No more interviews.

KATHARINE HEPBURN

Employees come and go, some sooner than others, but it is important to interview well and reduce the number of times you have to go through the hiring process. To increase your success rate, do not commit what I call the Seven Sins of Recruiting. Instead, follow the Three-Tier Selection Process to find your perfect candidate.

There are seven common mistakes that business owners and recruiters do wrong when recruiting, and if you commit any of them, you will be hiring again sooner than you would like to be.

1. Hiring by using the old format of job description alone. This will guarantee mis-

alignment between the employee personality traits and you.

2. Hiring on education and experience without testing the actual skills. If the position requires particular skills, then you need to know whether the applicant actually has these abilities. Where possible, have employees perform tasks in order to assess their skills.

3. Rushing the selection process. Haste = Waste. If you need someone now, then hire a temp while you are looking for the right person to join your team for the long term. Otherwise, a hasty hiring decision may lead to regret down the road.

4. Falling in love with the potential of a canidate. It is very easy to see what we want to see in a candidate and not see the true person for who they are. This is why it is important to engage in task-testing and reference checks.

5. Not inviting other employees to be part of the interview process. People will act differently toward their bosses than towards their coworkers. You want to ensure that you get input from the people who would actually

be working closely with your potential applicant. After all, group cohesion is a large factor in productivity.

6. Using computer algorithms. Recruiting agencies and large business sometimes try to reduce the number of applicants they need to personally review by using computer algorithm programs to remove unsuitable applicants based on factors like education, experience, and abilities that they believe do not fit their criteria. The problem with using algorithms is that savvy candiates can hire specialised resume writers to overcome these computor programs. Remember that people are more than just a maths equation, so you may accidentally be eliminating a great candidate that is perfect for the job just because they are not a computer cookie cutout.

7. Not knowing your leadership style and your business. You need to hire employees that work well with your style of leadership and the type of business you are building.

Instead of falling victim to these common mistakes, use a Three-Tier Selection Process that has seven easy steps. It's recommended that if you are just starting out and have no employees yet, that you enlist a close friend or family member to act as a sounding board. An extra pair of eyes and ears will help you in the journey of employing your first employee. If you have employees or prefer to use a reciuting agent make sure that you have trained them in the Three-Tier Selection Process.

The Three-Tier Selection Process will reduce the likelihood that you will hire the wrong staff. Hiring the wrong person can cost your business up to 2.5 times the salary of that employee and result in a 39% decrease in productivity. No small or medium size business can afford this cost.

The Three-Tier Selection Process

Firstly know who and what you want. Prepare a Task, Ability and Attitude Brief and, if applicable, develop a task test for the position. Either write the position advertisement or enlist a recruiting agent. Accept applications for 2-4 weeks. Set aside time in your calendar after the application closing date to do an initial review of the applications and allow a lot time in your calendar for interviews.

There are various ways to advertise the position, including:

1. Your business's social media sites and groups
2. LinkedIn and LinkedIn groups
3. Newspapers and industry magazines
4. Job-seeker websites
5. The entrance or front reception area of your business

Tier one—Culling the candidate list

Phone all candidates. You, an employee or a recruiting agent can complete this process by phoning all the applicants. Be sure to call every single one, as it will weed out up to 80% of the candidates and save you copious amounts of time by not having to check references or interviewing the wrong person. This is a five-minute phone call—simply thank the candidate for their application and ask just one question: 'What do you know about our business?'

This direct and simple question will tell you if they have done any research on your business. Asking this question will allow you to assess whether they're truly interested in working for you.

If they do not know who you are, they are probably floaters and most likely not keen to be part of your business in the long term. Do not proceed any further with the call; instead, thank these candidates for their time.

If they do not answer their phone, leave a message for them to call you back at a specific time or day. Follow this message up with an email to cover all contact bases, giving the applicant every possible chance to contact you. You may be surprised at how many applicants do not return your call or take a long time to do so. This will weed out the tyre kickers, time wasters and lazy applicants.

When you talk to the applicant, remember this is the first tier of the interview process, so don't chat for more than five minutes. Your time is valuable, and this step is designed to help you create a shortlist of applicants who you want to take to the next round.

During the phone call, note how the respondent talks about your business. Do they use 'I see', 'I hear', 'I've done' or 'I feel'? This will tell you if the candidate has a sight, auditory, action, or feelings-based personality. This simple analysis is the first step to determining the candidate's predominant learning and interaction style and this will match your leadership style. If you like what they have said, ask the applicant if you could call their references and their current/past employers. Remember that you should not talk to a candidate's current employer if they have requested you not to do so as it could jeopardise their current employment.

Thank candidates for their time and say that you will be in touch soon. For those candidates who are weeded out at this stage you should send an email confirming that they have been unsuccessful in the application process.

Analyse the results of the phone call and choose your top five-to-ten applicants. Take time to do your due diligence to ensure that you hire the right person for the job. Rushing to hire will only lead to choosing the wrong person. It is very important to complete the reference and background checks to determine the authenticity of their resumes. Call the candidate's referees who will likely provide information about the candidate's positive traits and their work history. You might also ask permission if you can call current/past workplaces to speak with previous co-workers. At the end of this chapter is a list of sample questions to ask the referees.

The final investigative task before making your preferred candidate list is to take a look at the applicant's online presence. This includes professional pages like LinkedIn, Google searches and any other public social media pages. Look for any red flags that suggest this candidate may be contrary to what you are looking for in an employee.

This thorough investigation will result in a shortlist of two-to-five candidates to take to the next level of interviews. Call them and set up the first face-to-face interview before emailing the unsuccessful applicants. Don't email the unsuccessful applicants until you have secured interviews with your top applicants. Some or all of those preferred candidates may have found other employment and you will have to revise your list.

" There seems to be some discrepancy between what you say in your CV and what you say on your Facebook page."

Tier two—the first interview with task test

This is the time you get to meet your preferred applicants in person, so the most important part of this interview is to ensure that the candidate will fit into your organisation and perform the tasks that you require. Conduct a task test to see if the applicant can walk the talk. The task test should be simple; specific to your business needs and be achievable within 30 minutes. Performing a task test as part of your application will reveal the candidate's attitudes plus demonstrate the abilities that they have highlighted in their resume.

Example of task test

If you are hiring a bookkeeper/accounts staff, give the applicant a shoebox of receipts to sort and put into a spreadsheet, or give them a trial balance sheet and get them to produce a profit and loss or cash-flow report.

If you need an administrative employee to do filing—set them a filling task.

If the position is for an engineer or designer have them to design a shed out of limited materials or analyse a construction drawing.

If the position is for a graphic artist, then have

the applicant design a simple pamphlet with copy provided.

The task testing is a very quick way to examine their skills and attitude firsthand.

Depending on the size of your organisation, you may conduct a formal interview with a selection panel made up of co-workers that will be directly working with the successful applicant. Allow the selection panel to ask as many questions as they want. However, it is important to keep the interview to under an hour. At the end of this chapter are sample questions that can be used for a formal interview.

When you and your employees are interviewing the applicants, it is important that you inform the candidates about your business, the work environment, the business culture and expectations, the type of boss you are and the salary package and incentives for the position.

Take notes during the interviewing process. Upon completions of all the interviews reflect on your notes and feedback from the selection panel. Take time to reflect on all the information and narrow your selection down to a short-list of no more than three applicants. Set up the final interview time for the top two or three candidates and send the unsuccessful candidates an email stating that they have been unsuccessful in the application process and thank them for their time.

Tier three—the final interview

Hold a casual interview with your top candidates. This is the secret weapon in selecting the best staff for you and your business. Many candidates can fake a formal interview and look fantastic on paper but take down these formal walls and put them in a casual environment, and you will see a different side to the candidates. The casual interview enables the candidate to drop their guard and it will expose the real person.

Set up a morning tea, lunch or a cocktail along with other employees who will be directly working these candidates. Explain to the candidate that you want to get to know them a little more without all the formalities of the work environment and formal interviews.

For the casual interview sit back and see what happens. Let the conversation flow, and allow the candidate to dictate where it goes. It is time for you to listen and observe how the candidate interacts with you and others.

Look for any red flags like foul language, inappropriate behaviour and information that contradicts what they have previously told you. Watch for how they interact with the people around them. The only rule with a casual interview is that it must stay casual, no serious talk about the business. If you find that the conversation is becoming too serious, cut in and change the subject to something more informal. For example, ask them about their last holiday or travel adventures, ask them about their favourite sports or hobby or even about their family. Keep it casual and relaxed.

Front desk position for printing company

Tanya and her team had narrowed the candidates down to two after the formal interviews and task testing. One candidate stood out; John, who was well dressed, personable and effectively put the focus on his customers. The other candidate, Sue, was extremely nervous in the interview and fumbled throughout the process, but she did show remarkable initiative in the task testing.

Although Tanya was leaning towards John, Tanya decided that before making a final decision she would have coffee with both candidates separately to help choose the right person for the position.

John turned up half an hour late and in a bad mood. Tanya ordered them both a coffee and reminded herself that everyone can have a bad start to the day. Tanya remained calm and remembered to sit back, listen and observe. When the coffee came, John did not make eye contact with the waiter or thank her. What came out in the conversation was eye-opening and the candidate never apologised or gave a reason for being so late. Tanya thanked the candidate for coming and said she would be in touch with her decision.

In contrast, Sue arrived for their coffee meeting on time, dressed in smart, casual. She apologised for her previous nerves and explained that she always freezes up in interviews.

One hour later, Tanya waved goodbye to Sue and sat back into the chair, taking a deep breath. She realised that she had just dodged a big bullet. Having coffee with the two candidates showed their true colours. Tanya hired Sue and never regrated her choice.

Before offering anyone a position, complete a post-mortem with your selection panel employees that were at the formal and casual interviews; and together choose the top candidate.

Offer your top candidate the position and cross your fingers that they accept. If they accept, only then do you send an email telling the other candidates that they were unsuccessful. If they do not accept, you can offer the position to the second-choice candidate or start the process again. Once the candidate has accepted the position, send them all the human resources (HR) forms to be completed before their start date. Do not forget to email the unsuccessful candidate

Although somewhat extensive, the Three-Tier Selection Process may be, this process will guarantee ensure that you only hire candidates who fit your leadership style and is perfect for your business.

Take-Home Point

Bad employees cost businesses millions of dollars every year. Don't commit the Seven Deadly Sins of Recruiting. Using the Three-Tier Selection Process will see the right staff shine through.

Sample Questions for References Checks
What is the nature of your relationship with the applicant?
In what capacity is/was the applicant employed by your business?
What were the dates of their employment?
What duties and responsibilities does/did the applicant have?
What was the applicant's reason for leaving?
What is the nature of your relationship with the applicant?
What makes the candidate a good fit for this job?
How would you describe the applicant's overall work performance?
What would you say are the applicant's strengths?
What would you say are the applicant's challenges?
Can you comment on the applicant's: • Reliability and punctuality • Attendance and Professionalism • Work with their co-workers and management
What advice can you give me to successfully manage the candidate?
Would you re-employ the applicant? Why/why not?
Do you have any final comments?

Formal Interview Questions:
What attracted you to this company?
What can you do for us that other candidates can't?
Why are you leaving your present job?
Give me an example of a time that you felt you went above and beyond the call of duty for a customer/client/stakeholder.
What is your greatest failure, and what did you learn from it?
A recent article said the most employees steal approximately $10 a week from their employers. What do you think about this article's findings?
How would you describe your work style?
What would be your ideal working environment?
If you had to choose one, would you consider yourself a big-picture person or a detail-oriented person?
Who was your favourite manager and why?
What do you think of your previous boss?
What kind of personality do you work best with and why?
What three character traits would your friends use to describe you?
List five words that describe your character.
What are the qualities of a good leader? A bad leader?
How do you feel about taking 'No' for an answer?
How many times do a clock's hands overlap in a day?
Tell me ten ways to use a pencil other than writing.
If you could choose one superhero power, what would it be and why?

Take Action and Let Go

Let them 'do' and become part of the team

> *You must be a lazy man if it takes you
> ten hours to do a day's work.*
>
> ANDREW CARNEGIE

Once you've hired your new employee, it is time to see how they work as an employee. Remember that the new employee will also be assessing your business and management style during the initial weeks and months.

It's important to help new employees transition smoothly into their position and into your business. Here are some suggestions of things that you could do to welcome your new employee and help break down any barriers and integrate them into your company's culture.

Have a welcome package ready. Your welcome package may include company promotional items—pens, mugs, chocolates—or a muffin and tickets to a movie or football game. This welcome package is meant to be fun and inviting. You should know enough about who the new employee is to make this welcome package a thoughtful gift.

Do not include employee's business phone numbers, procedure manuals, or other materials that are business-oriented. Such material should have been part of the HR pack sent before the employee's start date. You want your employee's first day to feel welcoming and fun, and a small welcome package can go a long way towards making a good impression.

Assign another employee to show the new employee around. Don't dump them at a desk with a computer and no guiding hand. It's nice to have someone who can help the employee get settled, and it helps them see your inclusive attitude.

Take the time to have a morning tea to introduce your new employee to all the other employees. This is a great ice-breaker and enables the new employee to feel welcome when they meet those they'll be working with.

Follow up with the new employee regularly during the probationary period, or until they feel that they are a part of the team. It is during these follow-ups that you should take the time to ask them how they are going. See if they need anything to ensure that their transition into your organisation is as smooth as possible.

Be careful not to create a negative impression of your company, especially during the probationary period. Do not forget that you are under probation as much as they are. There are a number of things that bosses often do that annoy new employees and make them want to leave immediately:

Being disorganised from the beginning. There is nothing worse than turning up to start work for a company and having no workspace or equipment prepared. Disorganisation gives the new employee a feeling that you are in chaos or that they are not needed or wanted.

Not personally welcoming the new staff member on their first day. The lack of a personal greeting will leave the new employee feeling like that they are just another cog in your moneymaking machine. It takes just five minutes of your day to welcome the new employee. I personally cannot think that there is any excuse for not taking the time to get to know your new employee and help them feel part of your team.

If you are out of town, then make a phone call

or organise a greeting card—a welcome note via email will seem far less personal and will not have the desired effect. Ask yourself what type of employee is going to work harder for you: a person that feels wanted in their new work environment, or a person that feels insignificant in the scheme of your company? It doesn't cost much time or money to make your employees feel welcome.

Not delivering on what was promised in the interview. Whether you guaranteed a particular office, a type of computer, or a specific pay rate, you need to stay true to your word. If you do not deliver what you have promised, then your new employee won't see you or your business as trustworthy. You don't want a new employee to reconsider their choice to work for your company.

After you have given the new employee time to settle in and have ensured that they have all the resources they need to succeed, then it is time to get out of their way. Let them do the task that you have employed them to do. This is the time for your employee to walk the walk and meet those KPIs.

Studies show that autonomy is one of the critical aspects of enabling employees to be happy at work. Below is a primary table showing how a boss with any leadership style can allow employees to have autonomy over their own work, and deliver accordingly. Use this table as the basis for formulating a more comprehensive table that is in line with your individual Boss Blueprint.

General Boss/Leadership Style and Staff Autonomy	
Control Enthusiast	You have given you new employee a detailed list of tasks, meetings, and reporting that is required for their position.
Visionary	You have outlined the completed tasks that you want to see and clarified who the new employee can go to if they need further guidance.
Coach	You have given the game plan and clarification on the employee's role in the team. You've told the employee what tasks they must complete to ensure that the group is able to reach the company's goals.
Commander	There will be daily, weekly and monthly tasks to be completed. You've informed the employee that they will be required to perform unscheduled tasks while meeting their normal requirements.

Letting your employees do what you have hired them to do is imperative when you have hired a specialist. Hiring intelligence is one of the most direct ways to build a company's success, employees that have skills beyond your own. You may have hired them to solve a problem or because they have expertise in a field that you do not. By hiring someone with more skills and talent in an area that you have, you get several benefits. Your business will gain a new set of ideas and new energy to the company to help you grow and prosper, you do not have to learn what they know, and you are free to do what you know and are best at doing.

Take-Home Point

Let your staff do what you employed them to do.

It's Me, Not You!

Breaking up can be easy

The first step to getting what you want is to have the courage to get rid of what you don't.

ZIG ZIGLAR

You may not even realise it, but you and your business could be losing customers, productivity and money because of the employees that you have hired. In this chapter we will determine what makes a bad employee and weigh up your options as an employer. We'll also examine how to remove bad staff without the fear of repercussions.

Who and What Make a Bad Employee?

Identifying employees who drain productivity and slow your business growth is the first step to finding a solution. There are seven types of employees who regularly cause problems for your businesses:

The invisible employee

This employee is never around when you are looking for them. They are constantly arriving late for work, leaving early and sneaking away at midday for long lunches. Irregular attendance might be a sign of a range problems, including issues at home, family commitments, illness or relationship breakups. Talk with this employee privately to find out what is triggering this irregularity. If the problem is of a private nature try to find a solution that works for both the troubled employee and your business, but if you find that it is job dissatisfaction, it warrants investigation and solving immediately.

The nonconformist

These are rebels without a cause who are determined to break the rules, from the simplest to the most complex. They often do so to the detriment to the business and its safety. Legally speaking, an employee who engages in reckless behaviour, such as driving dangerously or drinking on the job, should be removed from the workplace and investigated immediately.

Do not engage in power struggles with destructive non-conformist employees that see the workplace rules as controls. They may come across as a know-it-all, refusing to listen to instructions and instead choosing to do things their own way. Given enough time, this type of toxic behaviour can diminish your leadership and control of your business. A destructive non-conformer can take a toll on employee morale, and other employees may begin to wonder why they have to follow the rules when others don't.

A constructive nonconformist is simply an independent thinker who wants to make a difference in your workplace. Rather than just following along with what others tell them, they test and push boundaries to see if they can improve the workflow and grow your business. If you identify the employee as an independent thinker, utilise them to resolve issues in your business and have them identify why they choose to do things differently and how it is going to improve the business.

The drama queen

There is a drama queen in almost every group of people. They are individuals that live life as though it was a reality tv show or soap opera. They make things all about them. Their behaviour behind-the-scenes is often negative and divisive in tone, full of gossip and hearsay. They can also lead other employees to feel that their personal conversations are being monitored, creating a sense of distrust and negativity. This will hurt the social atmosphere in your workplace and diminish productivity.

The backstabber

These are negative employees who bad-mouth the company, other staff, customers and even the boss to others including fellow employees, customers and suppliers. They simply disrupt the morale of the business. They are discontented employees who need to be confronted and stopped.

"Well that team building weekend could have gone better!"

The thief

Whether stock is disappearing, the cash drawer doesn't add up, or an employee is stealing valuable information, theft can threaten your company's bottom line. Take immediate action to investigate and remove the employee immediately.

The victim

This is the employee that most bosses find particularly difficult to manage. The victim avoids accountability for their own actions, preferring to blame others for bad situations and come up with an excuse for everything. They have a list of ailments, injuries, illnesses and childhood drama they will parade out if cornered or asked to explain their unfavourable work level and productivity. The primary issue is that it will affect teamwork, cooperation with other employees and the business as a whole.

The person that does not fit your Boss Blueprint

This is the employee that just does not suit you or your business. Many small to medium sized businesses tend to hire based on what they need to be done right away, and thus employ a person whose skills and experience that only meet immediate business needs. However, people that can do the task now may not necessarily have the ability to grow their skills with the business.

Also, while they may be able to do the task at hand, they are causing you stress and are just a square peg in a round hole. After going through the exercises in this book you are now aware of the types of employees that suit your leadership style, and the others that need to be set free. It is okay to be honest about who you want to have work for you, always remember that this is your business, your dream and your future. I have found when I have said to an employee that I am the worst boss for them, and holding them back from finding a boss that suits them better, their reactions was one of relief. It opens up a dialogue between you and the employee to find a solution was.

Outgrown Employee

At a business marketing seminar I was talking to a business owner, Nina, who had started her health and exercise company from scratch just two years previously She told me that she was having a problem managing one of their employees to be more proactive in his work tasks and improve his time management as a receptionist/administrator.

The biggest complaint Nina had was that this employee would sit around and wait for instructions and could never see tasks that needed to be done and do them. This, despite the fact that many of the tasks were responsibilities that were part of his daily routine.

The first question I asked Nina was, did you used a task test during the interview stage? She said that the company hadn't done a task test due to lack of computers or an office at the time of the interview.

Next, I asked whether the positives of this employee outweighed the negatives. Nina reflected on this question and said that his saving grace was that he was always there to fill in if the other receptionist/administrator could not work due to sickness or holidays etc. The negative was the constant need to tell him what he needed to do next, EVERYDAY.

Then I asked Nina if the employee suited here management style? The answer was a resounding NO. Nina's management style was very much a hands-off approach. She wanted a work environment set up with tasks and expectations, and then let the employees self-manage.

Nina had provided further training and incentives to fix this constant problem but was running out of patience and options to help this employee to improve and suit her Boss Blueprint.

Finally, I asked 'If it was easy to fire this employee, would you?' Nina's reply was a unequivocal 'OH YES; I would've fired him months ago'.

When asked what was keeping her from firing him and getting a more suitable person to do the job, Nina replied with the following excuses:

1. *The business is so busy.*
2. *I could train him more.*
3. *What if I cannot find a better employee than what I have now?*
4. *How will I handle it if he bad-mouths me or my business?'*

All that stopped her from letting an unsuitable employee go were fear-based excuses, which was to the detriment to her business and stress levels. It was time for Nina to learn how to fire

> *bad staff and realise that her business would flourish without this staff member. Your business deserves the best employees.*

Taking action

Once you discover you have a problematic employee, it's critical to take action instead of letting it fester. As a general rule, direct and clear communication is the key. This is your business, your baby, your dream and your life. If you continue to allow bad employees to stay in your company, all you are doing is adding to your headaches, reducing productivity, affecting your work environment and reducing your profit margin. The bottom line is they have to go, and the sooner you remove them, the better it is for you and your business.

There are many reasons why you may have bad employees. You have made mistakes when hiring, or the job requirements have changed and the position has outgrown the employee's capabilities. Perhaps you may have inherited the employee when you bought the business. Too many businesses hold on to bad employees for far too long, like a bad romantic relationship. Too many bosses think if they pump more into the relationship, like training, motivational talks, empathy; that these actions will turn the person around and fix the problem. If you ask yourself, would you fire the person if you could do so easily and the answer is yes, then it is time to step up and learn the skills needed to be able to set the employee free.

The problem is that most people don't like conflict. We tend to bury our heads in the sand and hope the pain will go away on its own. Sometimes, the whole termination process intimidates bosses: the forms, the final payout, the shame of hiring the wrong person or avoiding the hiring process. Some bosses are afraid of being sued and accused of unfair dismissal. These are all valid concerns, but are these worth the price of stress, and losing good employees? Is it worth losing clients and sales just because you want to avoid confrontation? Why prolong the pain for both of you? Set the employee free; give them an opportunity to find a job that they love and where they are motivated to be their best. Think of it freeing them like a mother eagle pushing her baby out of the nest and off the cliff to learn how to fly. It is a hard thing to do, but in the end the baby learns to fly.

If you are terminating an employee's employment due to theft, violence, corruption, cheating or unsafe work practices, do it immediately once you have fully investigated the serious misconduct. Firing an employee on serious misconduct should be done loud and proud to ensure that all other employees know that these behaviours are not tolerated and that if found guilty of these acts, they will lose employment immediately. When I say loud and proud I do not mean that you announce it over a loud speaker but you do not makeup a coverup story. Simply when ask why you fired the employee, say that it was due to a grave misconduct and leave it at that.

If firing someone for other reasons, the most direct way to handle the terminating an employee is to set up a meeting. Give the employee a short, valid reason as to why you are terminating their employment with empathy and kindness. Say that you are sorry and inform them as to when their final pay will be paid, ask them to gather their personal belongings and wish them luck in the future. Simple. Job done and dusted. It is that easy.

But let's face it: if you were able to do the above without much trouble, you would have done it already. The best way I have found to remove unwanted employees from my companies is via a much gentler approach.

The most effective way to help an employee either move on or improve their work ethics very quickly is to use a method that I call the Reflective Mirror Method. It is a quick five-step process that works every time, usually without fuss, anger or repercussions.

The Reflective Mirror Method

Make a list of all of the employee's positives and negatives attributes. Then think about the reason why you hired them and what potential you saw in them at that time.

Arrange to have a meeting with the employee. I find that this works best on Thursday afternoons, about 30 minutes before the end of the day.

At the meeting, talk to them about all the positive traits that you initially saw in this person, including things that they currently do and what they bring to the company.

After you list positive attributes, say, 'I saw all this potential and believed that you were capable of …. (list the skills and abilities that they are not displaying currently which are needed for them to keep their job)'.

You always state the behaviour that you want to see the employee to display. This way, you have not accused your employee of any wrongdoing or said anything bad about them. Through this approach, you will ensure that the employee doesn't go on the defensive, start arguing or accuse you of being unfair or unjust.

How to frame things in a positive light

> Example 1—if you noted that an employee has become quiet, lazy and slow to complete tasks, instead of saying to them that they are lazy and doing below average work. you could say, 'When we first met, I thought you were energetic and had a lot of get up and go. You presented the ability to complete your tasks on time and at a high standard'.

> Example 2—if you found that an employee has been taking credit for other people's work, instead of pointing this out you could say, 'When we first met, I saw you as a person that was honest and fair and always gave credit where credit was due'.

The final step of the Reflective Mirror Method is to look the employee straight in their eyes and say, 'I do not think I was wrong about what I saw in you'. Pause, reflect, and the add, 'but maybe I was'. Go on to say, 'I would like you to take tomorrow off on full pay and think about whether you are happy here and if you can live up to the vision I have of you. Come Monday, I hope you come back and step up to the vision I have of you'.

Using the Reflective Mirror Method, it will likely lead to one of the following three outcomes:

Outcome 1—the employee just doesn't return on Monday. If they do not return, send the employee an email expressing your sadness and wish them well in the future. Then, it's time to complete their final pay and exit paperwork.

Outcome 2—the employee returns on Monday with a new zest and commitment to the business and their career. They become the employee you wanted them to be.

Outcome 3—the employee returns on Monday and tries to be the employee that you want, but ends up handing in their letter of resignation by the end of the week (90% chance of this happening).

If the employee returns on Monday, make sure that you take the time to go up to them and thank them for returning. Tell them that you look forward to continuing working with them and that you are happy to see them back.

The advantage of the Reflective Mirror Method

is that it provides the employee the opportunity to leave gracefully on their own terms. It avoids the messy and ugly process of a formal termination process. It reduces the chances of any unfair dismissal action and is freeing both of you with dignity.

One day, you may be lucky enough to have an ex-employee send you a note or call you to thank you for giving them the nudge they needed to find a job better suited to them and their skills. This is a wonderful feeling.

Take-Home Point

The old saying is that you catch more flies with honey than vinegar. This is certainly true when you want to see a positive change in an employee or want them to realise that it's time that they depart from your business.

Chapter 10

It's You, Not Me

It is never about the money

Experience is simply the name we give our mistakes.

OSCAR WILDE

Sometimes, it's not the boss who decides to end the employer-employee relationship. it is the employee that leaves you. More than once, I've stared into my coffee numbly as I listened to my best employee tell me that they were moving on to greener pastures. At times like these, you may question your leadership abilities. Don't sit there and keep bashing yourself, take the opportunity to look at why your employees are leaving and get to the heart of the problem.

Employees quit their jobs for many reasons. Sometimes, it is to move to a new town or to stay home with children. It could be a change in career path; to go back to school or to transfer to another company that enables them to move up the corporate ladder. Those reasons are hard to address for any boss, as they are not caused by problems within your business. Before the employee leaves your company, have them complete an exit form or interview. Otherwise, you are missing out on the opportunity to make some positive changes to your business that may benefit you and other employees.

" Okay... I think that concludes the exit interview."

An exit interview enables you to get information about your leaving employee's experience working for your company. This is particularly valuable considering that when an employee resigns, it's usually the last step in a much longer course of events and highly likely they have been considering leaving you for a while. It is time to look at any internal factors that may have driven them towards resigning. Find out if there are any courses of action you can take to prevent more employees from resigning. An exit interview provides insight into what an employee sees as a problem within your business.

The Attitude to Have When an Employee Leaves You

Toni owns several restaurants and businesses. His core belief is to ensure that every dining experience a customer has makes them feel welcome, with delicious food and a memorable occasion. He lives by the motto 'work hard, play hard'.

Toni had learnt not to take an employee leaving to heart— it's part of being in business. He knows that some employees may find his core values hard to meet, but he will not compromise them or reduce the experience for his customers.

He believes that he can turn a good chief into a great chief, but he cannot change a lazy non-interested person into an energetic, passionate

> *person; this quality must come from within the employees themselves.*
>
> *When an employee leaves the business, he sees it as a positive, as it frees him to improve the business if it requires it. He truly believes the departure allows his ex-employees to find a place that better suits their personalities and work ethics.*
>
> *Toni's attitude is, 'No Stress, this is part of being in business.'*

Although employees are not always a good fit for the business, it's best to minimise factors that would make employees want to leave. You never want to lose good employees, and you want your workplace to be somewhere that employees would want to spend their time.

Most of the time, people cite money as the reason for leaving, but there are often other factors that cause people to resign. It has been proven many times that the number one reason why people leave their job is that they are no longer happy. The most common reasons for employment unhappiness are:

1. The business environment.
2. Bullying or discrimination.

3. Corruption.
4. Unfriendly environment/ disconnect from other members of the workspace.
5. Overly-competitive environment.
6. The business vision sold to them in the interview didn't match the reality of the business.
7. Workload unevenly distributed.
8. Not feeling appreciated or recognised for their contributions.

All of these factors are part of the culture of the business. The way your company treats its employees and the way employees treat each other makes a big difference in employee happiness. You may have employed staff according to your Boss Blueprint, but this doesn't mean that you have developed an advantageous business culture.

A company's culture is evident in the business stories, routines, practices, and symbols of the business, which manifest from the company's working environment. The culture is shaped by who is controlling power, the formulation of policies and the structure of the business. For example, the defence force has a culture of mateship and is authoritarian. A government department is usually highly hieratical and silo in structure.

When you have a healthy productive culture,

you'll be able to maintain happy employees and reduce staff turnover. A great business culture will increase company loyalty and attract great talent leading to 20-30% better company performance.

There are some business cultures that can lead to unacceptable behaviours, which in turn ruin your workplace for other employees. For both the Australian Wheat Board and Leighton Holdings, the business culture was found to be the blame for kickbacks and corruption by all levels of management. The cover up within the Enron Corporation, and the greed of the banking sector, were causative factors that led to the Global Financial Crisis.

To start building a productive and robust culture, a business needs a strong company vision, healthy core values and clear objectives. To create these things, ask yourself three fundamental questions:

1. Why do we do what we do?
2. What do we believe, or how do we do what we do?
3. Where do want this business to be in the future?

Use the answers to these three questions as the basis of your interview questions. You want your employees to know what they are signing up for, and you want them to want to be a part of your business and its future. If your new employees align with your culture and values, it's easier for everyone to move in the same direction together.

Example Answers to the 3 Culture Forming Questions of an IT Company

Why do we do what we do?

We provide our customers with the most innovative software products in order to reduce their need to waste time with customer service and support.

What do we believe, or how do we do what we do?

Honesty, collective problem solving, compassion, innovation

Where do want this business to be in the future?

We want to provide both general and customised apps and software for use in the customer support industry.

Ultimately your workplace culture is unique to your business and can be an important key to the hiring process. A candidate that is a great fit culturally, and genuinely excited about the business vision, will more likely stay longer and have the ability to grow into different roles as the company grows; compared to an employee that has the education and experience but has the wrong culture fit.

It is essential to collaborate with staff, management and stakeholders to adjust, add or delete elements of your business culture as the business grows. Ensure that your business culture is one based on honesty, inclusiveness and trust.

Take-Home Point

Create a business culture and use it to help you to build a successful business. A good business culture enables you to keep the right staff. Always prioritise attitude over skills and experience.

Chapter 11

I Have Your Back if You Have Mine

It is all about teamwork

The man who does not read good books has no advantage over the man who cannot read them.

MARK TWAIN

You have hired the right staff and moved bad or ill-fitting employees onwards. You understand the importance of building a great business culture. Now it is time to review how to build a great team that is productive, happy and a pleasure to work with.

" There's always one isn't there?"

Having employees is about building a team of people that will strengthen and add value to your business. Making a great team is similar to creating your business culture and environment. It is essential to put the time and effort into building a great team. There are several practical steps you can do to help you set your team up for success.

Research has proven that team building exercises can have a measurable positive effect on team performance. The better the team the better the output will be. The time you put into team building exercises will pay dividends when implemented correctly. For team building exercises to be successful, they must not be forced upon employees, be invasive or make them feel awkward. The five best team building exercises that a business can do are:

1. Shared meals—put on a morning tea or have a BBQ on a Friday afternoon, as this allows your team to have casual conversations in a comfortable environment. It also helps your employees get to know each other outside of work.

2. Physical activities—sport make for an excellent break from work, and it allows employees to work together and get physical exercise too. Choose a sports activity that is not too physically strenuous and enables all employees, regardless of their fitness levels or sporting prowess to participate. For example, bowling, baseball, dancing, or a photo competition that requires walking a designated track.

3. Volunteering—this activity enables the entire team to participate and feel proud of their accomplishments. Helping your community gives your team a sense of pride and is an incredibly rewarding experience that all can join. Pick a local charity, school or sports team that needs help and get your

team to work. Volunteering is not a donation tin at the front of the reception; it's about hands-on involvement.

4. Field trips—casual trips to the museum, art shows, sporting events or even a play can do wonders for helping your team relax and connect.

5. Professional development events—workshops, conferences and forums increase your team's expert knowledge and help them network with others. These events allow employees to meet and extend their contacts within the industry to which they can reach out to if they have a problem to solve in your business.

All these team-building activities have one goal in mind. It is to foster informal conversation to allow the team to get to know each other outside of their roles within the business. Non-work discussions are critical to creating a team that looks out for each other.

Google—Project Aristotle: What makes a Great Team?

In 2010 Google set out to determine what makes a successful team. They wanted to know why some teams excelled, while others fell behind. They named the study Project Aristotle, a tribute to the philosopher whose most famous quote is 'The whole is greater than the sum of its parts'.

Google recruited statisticians, organisational psychologists, sociologists, engineers, and researchers to help solve the riddle. After two years of studying 180 Google teams and conducting over 200 interviews, they analysed over 250 different team attributes. But there was no clear pattern or dream team algorithm. It was not until they studied the intangibles—the unspoken, unwritten rules and customs that governed the teams—did the researchers find the dream team formula.

The researchers found that what mattered was less about who was on the team and more about how the team worked together.

1. Dependability—team members got things done on time and met one another's expectations.

2. Structure and clarity—there were clear goals and distinct, individual roles within the group.

3. Meaning—the work had personal significance to each member of the team.

> 4. Impact—*the work task is purposeful and has positive impacts.*
>
> 5. Psychological safety—*everyone felt safe to take risks, voice their opinions, and ask judgment-free questions. Create safe zones so employees can let down their guard.*
>
> *Check out Google's Rework Page for more information. https://rework.withgoogle.com/print/guides/5721312655835136/*

What mattered most is building a team that trusts each other. In other words, great teams thrive on trust. Trust is developed by the practice of listening first. When you take the time to listen first, you show your team that you want to understand what they are thinking, feeling and saying. The practice of allowing everyone to take turns speaking in a meeting, without interruption, enables the team to understand each individual's strengths, weaknesses, and style of communication. When people listen to one another, everyone feels valued and trust starts to build.

Trust also comes from authenticity and empathy. Egos have no place in a team. Team members must be able to work together towards common goals, not sabotage one another or compete against each other. It is important that team members feel comfortable learning from one another and apologise to each other when necessary. It is vital that you, as a boss, recognise and praise the efforts of your team and the individuals within this team.

Richard Branson and Virgin Blue Australia

> *I was very fortunate to be invited to the launch of Virgin Blue Airlines in Australia. As with any launch, there were the various speakers, acknowledgments and awards during the night. At most events like these, the person that is publicly acknowledged is the manager or supervisor.*
>
> *Richard Branson did something very extraordinary, he thanked the managers and supervisors for their great work but took this one step further. Richard took the time to acknowledge and give awards to a variety of people in the lower ranks of the organisation. He singled out team members including a receptionist and a flight attendant. The astounding sense of unity that this extraordinary act created was obvious to the assembled guests. Sir Richard made his employees feel that he saw them as important members of his company, no matter what*

> *rank or place they held within the organisation. Through recognising the individuals, he contributed to the strength of his whole team.*

Whether you have just hired your first employee or you are adding to your team, take the time to welcome them. Allow them to show you what they can do for your business. Finally, continue building a team that fosters growth, trust and inclusiveness. Building your team will help your business and your employees prosper.

Take-Home Point

Foster and develop a great team environment. Recognise the efforts of the individual while supporting the growth of the team.

Chapter 12

Sharing your Toys

Pay, incentives and pay rises

*It is the sweat of the servants
that make their squire look smart.*

AMIT KALANTRI

Even when you have the right employees working for you, it's important to retain them and compensate them appropriately. Of course, wage/salary is the primary compensation that you can offer your employees, so it's important to go about it the right way.

There are several schools of thought regarding monetary compensation and incentives. The first school of thought is 'If you pay higher wages/salary than your competitors or the industry standard, this will motivate employees to do better, deliver more, and be more committed to the business'. Some studies have shown that this enables you to attract better quality candidates and helps your business thrive.

The problem with this school of thought is that it does not look at what other reasons an employee could be drawn to work for a business like yours. If money is an employee's only motivation for working for your company, then their loyalty will always be to the next the highest bidder.

If you wish to pay an employee higher wages, then make sure that they are able to deliver value to the business that is above and beyond the normal expectation for a person in their position. You cannot afford to be paying for diamonds and getting coal in return. Be clear and open with your employees about what is expected from them in return for the higher than average compensation. However, you should still have the yearly wage review to ensure that your employee's wages are not being eroded by external pressures like inflation, housing interest rates and the cost of living.

I don't believe in paying higher than the market value for any given job, especially in the first three to six months of the probation period. If an employee comes to me saying they have been offered a position that will pay them more, then I do not try to compete with the offer. If an employee has gone looking for another job with another company, then no amount of money is going to change their dissatisfaction with your company. Just set them free.

Another reward structure is to 'pay' an employee based on performance, not actual hours worked. If an employee can complete their task (to the expected standard and time frame) in less time, then reward them by letting them have the remaining time off. Employees can prioritise their work and become incentivised to streamline their tasks to meet the company's business needs. This incentive model gives employees more autonomy when it comes to managing workflow.

The second school of thought is to offer incentives that more directly appeal to employees. Here small to medium businesses may have the advantage over large companies as to what they can offer. You can make the incentives personalised so that the employee's actions directly influence the size and amount of incentives that they can achieve. This structure offers the employee autonomy over their whole wage package. Employee incentive programs don't need to be grand gestures or expensive; they need to be meaningful and genuine incentives that the employee truly wants.

"That's what I like to see on a Monday morning, a happy employee."

For example, you can offer employees flexible start and finish times to enable them to fit their personal commitments in and around their work responsibilities. They may start several hours earlier to miss the peak hour traffic, or they may start later so that they are free to take their children to school. As long as the employee can meet your business needs, then you can allow them the flexibility to determine the hours they start and finish work.

Employee incentive programs can include discounts with other local businesses. This incentive is a great way to support other businesses. Try approaching other local businesses and ask if they would be willing to give your employees a discount if they shop with them; offer to do the same for their employees. This not only benefits your employees but also increases your customer base.

Story of the Chocolate Biscuits and Employee Productivity

> *Companies that offer tea/coffee and biscuits to their employees (free of charge), are 5-10% more productive than companies that don't provide this incentive. However, if you do a cost-cutting exercise and remove the biscuits, productivity drops 5-10% below that of com-*

> panies that offer no free refreshments at all! Your productivity will drop between 10-20%.
>
> In simple terms, these food and drink items may cost a business $50 a week; if your sales employees normally generate $2000 a week and their productivity drops by 10-20%, then you are losing $200-$400 per week.
>
> It's interesting to note that if you reintroduce cookies back into the workplace, the productivity level never goes back to as high as it was prior to the cost-cutting. Your company may, if lucky, go to the level of companies that offer no refreshments. The reason for this is that the cost-cutting exercise has damaged your employees level of trust level.

Profit-sharing, a model in which every employee receives a percentage of the company's profit, is another way to structure incentives. Opening up your books and enabling employees to understand how their efforts affect the success and profit of the business can increase employee productivity and morale while decreasing staff turnover. One reason to offer profit-sharing in your business is to get everyone in the company aligned to the same goals.

Before you implement a profit-sharing plan, you'll want to consider every aspect of what this will mean: Which employees will be eligible for the profit-share? To what degree will profits be shared? When will employees be paid this profit?

A successful profit-sharing system requires:

1. Rewards based around behaviours that you want to encourage that will grow the business ethically and sustainably.
2. Being transparent about your company's financial information.
3. Setting clear, realistic expectations about what the company must achieve to enable the profit-sharing.
4. Clearly explaining how much employees can expect to receive.

Ricardo Semler—Profit-Sharing System.

In the book Maverick: The Success Story Behind the World's Most Unusual Workplace *by Ricardo Semler, the author discusses introducing a profit-sharing system that his workers could understand and benefit from. His business did the following:*

1. Produce financial reports in a simplified format.
2. Educated his employees on how to read these financial reports.
3. Explained why the shareholders and company owners must be paid and the importance of saving for a rainy day.
4. Allowed the employees to devise how the profit-share should be distributed to them.

Over the years, Ricardo Semler found that the profit-share was 1/3 for shareholder/owners, 1/3 for future investments and 1/3 to the employees. He also found that the employees distributed profit evenly to all members, no matter what position they held or how long they had worked for the company.

It is very important how you structure and implement a profit-sharing system. You do not want to build a business that over sells and under delivers or to have the sales team recommending products that customers do not need or want, as this will lead to your company having greater than average product returns or cancelled services. In the long run this will jeopardise the reputation of your company and produce a down turn of your profits.

It is also important to remember that profit is the result of the whole business and not just the dollar figure in a financial report. Cost-cutting for the sake of profit could diminish business effectiveness. Take the time to map out an incentive program. Make sure you consider your business's financial situation and your employees' lifestyles and habits before deciding on an incentive program.

When your business in in start-up mode or funds are limited due to growing the business, you need to remember not all incentives have to be monetary-based. An incentive can be a personal note from you showing your appreciation for the work that the individual employee is doing. You can conduct a yearly award program that recognises outstanding efforts or a mentoring program for employees that want to improve.

Another incentive scheme is to allow your employees to work on pet projects that could benefit both your business and them. Companies like 3M and Google have programs where employees can spend 20% of their time doing whatever they want. It may be having coffee with a co-worker, checking their personal email or social media or working on side projects that may or may not have financial gain to the company. I believe in rewarding excellence, creativity, and out-of-the-box thinking, so it is important that I allow my employees the time and freedom to be able to do this.

M3 and the Post-it

> *In 1974, M3's Spencer Silver was working on developing an ultra-strong adhesive for use in aircraft construction. Instead, a mistake led to the creation of acrylate co-polymer microspheres, which were weak, pressure-sensitive adhesives. This meant that the sticky substance could be peeled away without leaving residue.*
>
> *It was not until Art Fry used the reusable adhesive for his hymn notes in his church songbook that he suggested using the adhesives on the backs of paper so that they could be stuck and removed without leaving residue.*
>
> *Four years later, in 1977, the product was finally tested for real-world sales for the first time, with a limited launch in four cities to see if anyone would buy it. The test failed because it was new, and people didn't understand the value of the product.*
>
> *In 1978, a year after the flop the driving employee behind Post-it Notes tried to make their product a success one more time. They sent out*

large numbers of free samples to companies for them to try and then tracked how many of them re-ordered additional units. To many people's surprise, almost 90% of these companies re-ordered the product. And the rest is history.

Another non-financial incentive is discarding the traditional annual leave and sick leave system in favour of a pool of paid time off that employees can choose to use at their convenience. This incentive would require some regulation to prevent abuse. For example, you could institute a simple rule that a notice of leave must be lodged for approval a minimum of five days prior to leave, However, this is up to each and every business to find a balance to meet both the employees needs and the business legal and operational needs. This type of incentive would need to negotiated within the employment contract to ensure you meet your country's workplace relations laws.

Take-Home Point

We offer incentives to our employees to reward excellent, not average. Provide employees with inspiration, not motivation, as it has a lasting effect.

Back to the Future

Recap and where to go for help

The secret of change is to focus all your energy not on fighting the old but on building the new.

SOCRATES

Stepping out from a Lone Wolf and starting to hire employees will reduce your workload, your stress levels and will enable you to have a personal life and time to recharge. Hiring employees has many benefits but having the right personnel will take your business to the next level of success.

This book is about finding out who you are and understanding your leadership style. The personal journey of self-discovery is to enable you to recognise your Boss Blueprint. Holding up a mirror and being honest about your personality traits ensures that you are able to find the right staff for you and your business. I don't care if you are arrogant, naive, love hearing own voice or prefer not to talk to anyone until 10 am. Just know it and own it. Find your positive personality traits and work on any negative traits that are detrimental to you and your business. Along with understanding your personality traits, it is important to understand how you learn and problem-solve plus be aware of how your employees learn and solve problems.

Owning your Staff Learning and Problem Style to a Compatible Work Environment

Brenda had a small business but the chatter from her staff drove her mad. She could not understand how any of them were productive with all this talking. She just wanted them to be silent and do their work. Provided she has a view to gaze at, Brenda can work in silence for hours. Brenda is a sight-activated person.

From reading this book, you would now understand, just in this simple story, that Brenda had hired auditory personality types.

Without firing everyone and starting all over again, there are some simple steps Brenda could do to solve her problem. Having ascertain that the chatter is not affecting staff performance she could:

1. *Buy earplugs and make sure that her desk has a large image that she can gaze upon if she cannot face her desk towards a window with a view.*
2. *Playing music that filters throughout the office which would help reduce the chatter as it would meet her employees' auditory needs and also give Brenda respite from the noise.*
3. *Set up a system that alerts her staff for her need for quiet. when she is working on a task requiring intense concentration and silence. For example, she could don pink ear muffs or ring a bell. With a simple signal her employees would understand that they need be silent for the next hour or two. Most auditory people can cope for this amount of time without affecting their productivity.*

However if analysis of the employee's work shows that productivity is being reduced by the chatter, she needs to remind her staff of what needs to be done and when. This should be done without resorting to saying 'If you talk less you would get these task done'. The Reflective Mirror Method can be modified to its simplest format to help correct small staff performance issues.

It is essential to take time to reflect upon the foundation of your business, where you want to go to in the future, and then determine what task you need to be completed by employees, contractors or have the task outsourced.

By completing the Tasks to Your Boss Blueprint Exercise in cchapter 5, you will have designed a template to ascertain if you are going to have this work performed internally or externally, and you will know to what standard, and when, you want this task to be completed.

Hiring employees can be time-consuming and costly to your business, especially if you keep hiring the wrong people. The Three-Tier Selection Process will reduce the incidents of hiring unsuitable employees for you, and your company. The first tier of the process is to remove the time wasters and non-suitable candidates. The formal interviews, which include task testing, will qualify the top candidates to take through to the final selection interview. The final interview is unorthodox as it is carried out in a casual environment which puts the candidate into a relaxed mode and allows for their natural personality and qualities to shine through.

Once you have the right staff, it is important to build team dynamics and the culture of your business as this will dictate the overall feel of the company and how your business will move forward in the future. Great teams are not reliant on the diversity of the group but the intangibles; unspoken/unwritten rules and customs that govern the team which builds trust, reliance and resilience. Like team dynamics, the business culture has its personality, values, beliefs, and unspoken assumptions. It is the intangible factors that underline the actions of the company and the people in it, to fulfil the business vision and goals.

An Outstanding Business Culture—Southwest Airlines

> *Industrial upheaval, grumpy employees and poor customer service hampers the airline industry but there is one company that bucks those trends. Southwest Airlines is a shining light not only to its competitors, but also a glowing example of a high business culture that has unprecedented customer loyalty and fantastic employee retention.*

> The company has been in operation for over 40 years and has continuously been able to communicate the goals and vision that unites their workforce. Southwest's core culture values include: warrior spirit, heart-felt service and a fun-loving attitude, and the company prides itself on propagating this culture through its employees. Their culture is an integral part of their brand and the company fosters it time, money and respect.
>
> Southwest Airlines also gives their employees consent to go the extra mile to make customers happy. Southwest Airlines empowers their staff to do what they need to do to meet the company's vision to become the world's most loved, most flown, and most profitable airline through the highest quality customer service delivered with a sense of warmth, friendliness, individual pride, and the company spirit. Southwest Airlines honours employees who exemplify this cultural mantra through awards and events.

As with anything in life, there is the good, the bad and the ugly to being a boss. Managing employees can be particularly challenging in many ways. Firing an employee can be a hugely stressful experience for any business owner. It is the way you handle the departure of an unwanted employee that is the key to ensuring everyone walks away with dignity and respect. The use of the Reflective Mirror Method will, time and time again, enable a positive outcome to a potentially awkward situation.

You employees also have the right to free themselves of you if they no longer feel that you and your company fits with their dreams, ambitions and goals.

It is paramount for your business that you take the time to conduct an exit interview to quantify why employees are leaving and establish if there were internal reasons for their departure. Exit interviews will highlight if there are adverse cultural or team dynamics that you can rectify to prevent the loss of further employees and to strengthen your business.

This book's aim is to provide a set of tools that will make hiring and firing of employees more comfortable and less draining. Armed with this toolbox, you can better understand what type of boss you are and find and keep the right staff.

For templates and further information please go to www.therightstaffbook.com

www.ingramcontent.com/pod-product-compliance
Lightning Source LLC
Chambersburg PA
CBHW071922290426
44110CB00013B/1446